PRAISE FOR DOR

"You must write a self/ out of waiting/ to speak" asserts Alina Ștefănescu's *Dor* and oh, what a prismatic, many-headed self has been written into existence within these pages. In her stunning second full-length collection, Ștefănescu explores the worlds contained in the Romanian word Dor— a word close to longing but with no exact English equivalent—as it relates to the speaker's life as a daughter, a mother, a foreign body in a country that harms and holds us conditionally. Simultaneously tender and incisive, witty and full transformations, this book and its many ecosystems of longing and belonging begs to be re-read and promises new wonders each time.
— Jihyun Yun, author of *Some Are Always Hungry*, winner of the Prairie Schooner Book Prize in Poetry

In one of the beautiful poems in the collection, *Dor*, Alina Ștefănescu writes of a "heart shaped like a shovel." Indeed, Ștefănescu's heart unearths the rich mysteries of an amalgam of Romanian and southern American culture in language deeply shadowed but attentive to the most telling of details. This is a collection that twists form and content into poems that are by turns tender or incendiary, or both.
— Erin Coughlin Hollowell, author of *Every Atom*

Alina Ștefănescu's *Dor* is a compendium of desire, displacement, longing, and belonging. While the word "dor" itself "serves as a bridge which creates its own territory from fusion," here Stefanescu's words do their own act of bridging the spaces between the body and language. In these poems, tongues, like nations, have borders; nouns and verbs come alive with ownership and agency. Stefanescu writes "a good girl poem waits // for the bass." but these are not good girl poems. Part genealogy of influences, part meditation on love, lust, and loss, and part pointed feminist critique, *Dor* is a multi-faceted collection that creates a newly textured landscape of language.
— Emily Holland, author of *Lineage* and editor of *Poet Lore*

Looking at what makes her heart soar with *Dor*, Alina Ștefănescu leads us through undilluted layers of loss, love, time, language and identity, showing that "the verb for longing in Romanian is a mouth." The condensed nature of the poems and their wordplay invite the reader into a world of sensation and memory where language shifts and blooms, filling mouth and eyes with delight, where, "any body is a bow, tuned to tremble."
— Clara Burghelea, author of *The Flavor of the Other*

Some of the most complicated and haunting songs live inside these poems: nocturnes and fugues, the humming of wordless lullabies, birds who "sing in unpredatored darkness," and most significantly, the doina—a traditional Romanian folk song of intense longing. That longing charges and electrifies this book: an attempt to hold the uncontainable, to name the unnamable, to translate an emotion that can't quite be translated from one language to another. From inside these uncharted spaces, Alina Ştefănescu gifts us with this moving collection and all its rare, disquieting music.

— Matthew Olzmann, author of *Contradictions in the Design*

"And what is memory / if not fondled ache…" From the Romanian Republic of Alabama, "where longing is /a homeland", Alina Ştefănescu's *Dor* sings us back to the forgotten, the lost, the silences we hold and grow; here we learn, "looking back is a way of looking within." These are poems that bruise in the way they remind us we are alive, "The gentlest fugue begins in fear/ of loss, and develops its argument." Ştefănescu's poems are soaked in vinegar, "the sour that protects," and revolve always toward what "failure fails to kill us." We can't remove what is already lost; the goat replaced is still missing, the mother lost is still with us. In this book, we learn our contradictions and our limitations; "It is the absence / of wings that teaches us to walk." Writing us into this world, where a "city swallows whole stars" and "All executioners go home for supper," Ştefănescu has made a mirror; if we are vulnerable enough in this American light, we will look—for in this collection, "the muscles of letters leave / irresistible witness to the world." The book will singe your fingertips, show the life you are sewn into, feed you missing language, and cut through the deep-fake of not feeling. As the poet reminds us, "The danger is not dying but *living in exile from / longing*."

— Amelia Martens, author of *The Spoons in the Grass Are There to Dig a Moat*

DOR

POETRY BY

ALINA ȘTEFĂNESCU

Wandering Aengus Press
Eastsound, Washington

First Edition published by Wandering Aengus Press

Poetry
ISBN: 978-0-578-91578-4
Printed in the United States of America.
Author Photo: Patrick Coryell
Cover Art: Ioana Hobai, www.ioanahobai.com
Book Design: Jill McCabe Johnson

Wandering Aengus Press
PO Box 334 Eastsound, WA 98245
wanderingaenguspress.com

Wandering Aengus Press is dedicated to publishing works to enrich lives and make the world a better place.

Contents

DOR

+

Dor is an Aromanian verb used to designate the action of hurting or aching. *Dor* is a Romanian noun defined as a state of unsated longing or yearning.

+

Dor exists in the harmonic space where opposite feelings—pain and sorrow, seeking and not finding—meet. As a word, it serves as a bridge which creates its own territory from fusion which blends words rather than composing new ones by joining together two or more words as one sees in German. As such, dor is a fused state, a effusion with traces of fugues.

+

Dor denotes a complex spiritual experience, one that involves profound longing, the sorrow caused by the unfulfilled moment of that longing, as well as the acute awareness of the impossibility of that fulfillment. This bundle of seemingly contradictory feelings is marked by a tinge of pleasure, derived from the longing itself. It is often employed in a context of nostalgically summoning up, in one's mind, a temporally or spatially remote sense of well-being, a loved person, now absent, or some other previous experience of joy or bliss.

+

Etymologically, the word derives from the Latin *dolus*, which means pain.

The verb *a dori* (to want or desire) derives from dor.

[Because the available language does not make space for how the noun I am trying to bring into it modifies the space around it, many unusual word combinations may exist. These are dor-words....]

for my father, Doru, whose name is rooted in longing,
and who made a home for us there

I miss you like
missing words

I miss you
as if the act

is inherent in the naming
& maybe Romanian

is the only language

where longing is
a homeland

where longing is
so reliable

that mothers name
their sons Longing

to keep them
nearer

Early Doinas

A *doina* is a traditional Romanian folk song which originates in vocalizations from village culture. Used to convey longing for one's place or home, UNESCO has named doinas an endangered musical form, threatened by displacement, capitalism, and forgetting.

*

I believed a person could consider himself a human being as long as he felt totally prepared to kill himself, to interfere in his own biography. It was this awareness that provided the will to live.

Varlam Shalamov

Unamerican Litany

for your walls

Because I didn't hear how my parents fled Romania when
purple clematis stole my attention, I bless the loss (and the losing-

ness) now. Because the absence of certain stories haunts me, I bless my
grandfather's microscope, crafted to observe the tiniest verbs we imagine,

and flown in from Bucharest to rule our Alabama table, an alien resident
with cabbaged accent. Because love can be period costume, I bless the bodice

of unforgiven slights that stiffens our bodies, bless these undergarments
worn to guise this longing towards being stripped from a lyric in Tom

Waits' throat, or the random jawbone we never noticed in that part of
the yard we left our clothes. In this heart of taking things off (and for

the grace of your beard and a morning), I bless the pre-breakfast tantrum,
the after-school scowl, the tucking-in of all kinned mammals that bless us with

demands for terrible fables, soft puppies, tinfoil crowns. I bless the bed
that does not bless me with sleep, bless the broken-wicked candle, bless

the omnishambles of stars strangled by Birmingham lights. Because you return
from work, and failure fails to kill us, I bless the sidewalk with chalk, saying

You, dear sidewalk, are a beautiful molehill of countless rejections—and scribble
the rejectedness bright pink. Because the poem won't come, I bless the

boots I've worn to stomp out of the house I've become to hide from the mouse
inside every story I've written, only to pause, turn back, bless this

imminent rodent: the courage of its undesired presence, the persistence
of its tiny scratchings, the valiance of its wall-crumbling teeth.

PICKLED PLUMS

I dub them, those three
citizens of my womb, the ones

I didn't deport. Although I know
plums are hard to grow

on foreign soil. Plums are finicky,
unreliable, quick to revolt or

pout. Like my mother, I plant-
ed a Romanian plum sapling

in the northeast corner of
the yard to keep evil away.

Like my father, I take three
thimbles of *tuica* before dinner

to prepare the throat for
what the mouth may say.

COSMOLOGY

Charles Simic says old godheads are dead. From here to eternity, we must create our own cosmologies as we lie in bed at night. I hope insomnia leaves the world richer, thicker, more bisqued. My cosmos includes stories mom recounted in Romanian, Rilke read between slurps of cabbage soup, teen dreams who tucked me in, one tape cassette of Chopin's nocturnes, the thin skein of leftover toothpaste. How many know our place by the route plastic neon stars take across a ceiling? I painted my room dark blue in high school no color felt deep enough. A cosmos should include things coming to get me — the car crash, secret cancer blossom, uncanny plague of locusts, that terrible handsome prince, his tortured steed. One day I'll be old enough to marvel without terror. One day all known stars may come unstuck.

Doina for What They Did

New York Times, March 4, 1983: *Arthur Koestler, an archetype of the activist Central European intellectual who drew on his Communist background for the antitotalitarian novel "Darkness at Noon," was found dead with his wife at their London home yesterday. Police officials said their deaths were apparently by suicide....the police, alerted by a maid, found the bodies of Mr. Koestler, who was 77 years old, and his wife, Cynthia, believed to be in her 50's, seated in chairs in the living room of their home in the Knightsbridge section. The maid, Amelia Marino, had found a note instructing her to call the police.*

The wall had not yet fallen.
It was 1983, harbinger
or hope, depending.
I was new to the promise
of America, new to sharing
a full-size mattress with two parents
and a sister in a studio apartment
with no sofa or table or chairs.
I was new to being nothing, the older
sibling of sweetness protected
by an American name. She was our
anchor baby, the born-here child,
the singular citizen in a family of four.
My parents' struggle was not suicide but
its opposite, an effort at life as it lapped
the edge of almost dying, the near of
disappearing, the kin that could not
forgive them. What do monsters
sing to calm babies that fight
a cockroach for breadcrumbs?
What lullaby makes us human?
Nani, nani, pui-ul mamei....*
and mom's voice, delicate,
quiet as a hen who nests near
the molding omelet.

* *Lyric from Romanian lullaby meaning "mommy's baby chick"*

First Crush Doina

Father Constantine returns
from Mount Athos with ashes.

They are magic, he says, it's a mystery.

I am thirteen, ready to marry,
to pledge my dreams to a monk or nothing.
I am going holy or bust.

I want a spouse who can never
appreciate the world in me.

I want a simple fool who will leave
his girl for loose frankincense
or vespers.

I want his kind in all its variations:
an anchorite or cave-dweller who lives
inside a hole god blew into rock for
no reason; a stylite who perches atop
the capitol of a ruined temple to pray without
ceasing; a dendrite who chains himself
to the upper branches of a massive tree and sings
like a sparrow; a stalagmite that grows
up or goes down, depending
on heaven's whim.

I want Him to crush me.

I nourish this canyon in my head
for the man in a long black dress
who can't love me enough.

DOINA FOR OUR FIRST GOAT

The first goat to reside inside
Tuscaloosa city limits was mom's
Surprise — and dad's nightmare.

This horned citizen of the Romanian
Republic of Alabama cared little
for cars, leaving a trail of bullet-

breath feces through the garage
on his route to prestigious azaleas or
inflamed clover. The goat sang

doinas about the life he'd led before
the border. *Poor thing! He is bleating,*
my mom told the magnolia.

I tracked his mystical eyes, hoped
he wouldn't bleed to death in the yard
in full view of the flaggiest neighbors.

Dad stayed worried and upset. *You
did not ask my consent before bringing
a goat in the house*, he announced.

Mom laughed at his wrongness: *Doru,
the goat is only a naturalized citizen. His
entry has limits.* Bubbica* was an outside

pet. I remembered this last year when
my partner bloomed red as grave's faux
begonias. When he asked what wild earth

filled my head, what fresh nonsense led me
to buy a goat! O city! O neighbors! O poop-
beads necklacing the driveway! And that

moment one wants to hug the patriarch
without quite waiting for his consent.

* *The goat's diminutive, Bubbica, comes from combining one localism—Bubba—with a feature of the Romanian language which modifies the ending of any noun to make it "little" or precious. In a sense, everything can be endearing in Romanian; affection is a way of modifying the word rather than adding a list of qualifiers or adjectives. Love is inherent.*

Memorium for December 21, 1989

after Wang May (and with the words of whatever male mammal wrote John 19:30)

Enough of absence makes the heart
grow fonder. Enough of older ladies hollering
christmas-tinsel things from across the street.
Enough glossy green bunting drooling out
of mailboxes, each american house with its own
fill-me, fill-me-full mouth.
On the sidelines, a streetlamp flickers
then winks, twice. It partakes of holiday lighting
as comrade or communicant.
And that jolly, inflatable snow-
fellow, knocked over by a cat in the yard.
A constant ringing of phones and jingles.
The word *revolution* lying sideways
like the snowman
I remember.
A woman's voice weeping in Romanian,
saying *mama, s-a terminat.**

* *Means "it is finished" or "it is fulfilled" in Romanian.*

THE COMMUNIST AT CATHOLIC SCHOOL: A "MULTIPLE-CHOICE" TEST

I was the Communist at Catholic school, my flesh

    a)   a ticking bomb waiting to blow
    b)   the knot in our pink, plastic rosaries

I was the vanguard of Ceausescu's dictatorship when we studied
your cold wars. I was the agent with no agency

    a)   the result of their prayers to bring me here or else
    b)   the "They" who held babies in unimaginable orphanages

I was always whatever They said
because I was not born here & therefore
I was an unreliable narrator.

Like all Soviet spies serving silent indictments concurrently, I was

    a)   the lanky fifth-grader in bright red jeans, oblivious
    b)   to how each hop, skip, or jump instantiated a hammer
    c)   every twirl or giggle set forth a sickle

When my long division looked funny, the teacher nodded grimly:
"It's because they do things differently *over there...*"

Over there was a murky, hereditary somewhere:

    a)   sometimes my family's suburban house
    b)   frequently a country called Ro-*mania*, the word whispered so softly
    c)   it disappeared among auditoriums of raised eyebrows

There were clues that I failed to conjugate in how capitalist girls smelled of
hot plastic barbie, after-school sitcom, polyester gym shorts
strawberry glossed kiss-me, eat-me gooeyness

The heritage of boiled cabbage clung like extended family
to my clothing, the scent of elders & kids crammed in kitchens,
talking their way around glass canning jars.

You can smell refugees from the way their stories pickle,
from the sourness they leave on the tongue

  ["*Da*, but it's the sour that protects; vinegar preserves
the vegetables. *Aşa se face.*"]

It must have been awkward for loyal teachers, students, school staff
keeping the national-insecurity secret that I was

   a)   commie, an inevitable product of my parent's defection
   b)   missing link in Marx's international wing of dialectical materialist
   c)   legal alien who lunched from paper napkins spotted by oil

I didn't know yet that looking back is a way of looking within

   a)   scouring blood for the contaminations of iron-fisted DNA
   b)   scouring words for deviations
   c)   scouring the sky for a planet where humans lived whole

Everyone is so kind to immigrants here, no one draws a clear line
from the incense of native tongues to the Kremlin

So I tried, keep trying, pledge to marry that flag & never
cook lentils two nights in a row, groom myself for the market,
consecrate the meritocracy, its self-esteemed experts

explain me again. The choice of translation is for the chosen

not for the nation of commies vampires orphans
hiding within

a single girl who wasn't & isn't

I mean never have I ever been
catholic.

ME & THE KING

In a Transylvanian village
they speak of a king

who laughs with one eye
and weeps with the other.

He keeps me company in these canyons
between city buildings.

Did you sob after losing your blue
notebook in Manhattan?

I cry with one eye
and lie with another.

Sleepwalk the subway to Coney Island
seeking a mermaid to recover

my story. At least one way needs
mermaids to end things.

One train needs to catch its own breath
at the end of the world we

won't remember
losing. Because the sky is too much—

the sky is a certain fire when
the poet accuses,

the podium weeps.

PLAYING POSSUM

This is my mother, newly-dead, Mom says. *She died without suffering.*

I fondle the photo of my maternal grandma playing possum.
A dead possum in a ditch is called *roadkill*.
A possum who's just playing is not yet *carcass*.
The women in my family will play anything to make you
wonder. Just to see what you'd say about us then.

The woman in the photo is my namesake.
The photo taken by the man she met and married in med school.
It was he who administered the final morphine injection
when breast cancer claimed her brain. He did this
without telling their daughters. He consulted none, invited

none into the living room of the Transylvanian cottage
he drafted and built by hand. It was her green dream-house.
He did it because she wanted to remain herself.
She made him *promise*. She made him promise again.

She said *if you love me….*

He signed her request with a blue fountain pen
from Czechoslovakia. The contract hid among papers, letters,
photos he preserved, images of her naked breasts, arms raised
above her head, his *Alina*, winsome, hungry, amorous,
and finally, finally, faceless….two gray hands

locked in languor over her chest. An orthodox cross
laid over v-shaped limbs, a flock of birds on their way to the Danube.

I am an atheist now, he announced.

But no one believed. None believed a man who hated god so faithfully
could ever come to disbelieve Himself. This was Ceausescu's Romania.
The dictator ruled from posters with iron fists. I know hate
and hope are kindred, knit through our palms. And these lines

in my hand: a silenced mutation.

"Like a Fire of Suspicious Origin"

after Nicole Sealey

And you who were named for death,
you follow the smoke towards a source, follow some flame
to explain the viciousness of gossip

that circles girl mouths like the perfect round
tin of a trash lid. Over the code words. Over the rotting
milk, the eyebrows rising like worms

over and over the words that hurt worse
for denial of them. There is no fire.
You are still nothing. No thing can

change. The smoke of your wild imagination
is inventing a forest. And you remain
stupid enough to look up,

to climb a tree trunk, believing that rising above
a source will protect you. There is no fire.
There is the base, smoldering.

The tree you climbed starts
its burn from the ground.

Dynamite

Keep on walking gentlemen, panic is a bad joke, here is the next number. The show goes on. The tickets are not reimbursable. Nothing is reversible. Nothing that has been will ever be again. At the last judgement only poetry will judge mankind. It alone did not lose man for even one second from its sharp sight. Who dares to raise up his head and set on the words? Man is an animal that poetry carves out from clay or blows up with dynamite.

Benjamin Fondane

Apologia

At 22, I disappeared for a minute.
I did not respond when you called me.

I wanted the death Alabama didn't offer.
I did not want the local D & C option. I refused
the twilight sedation, the succor of a specialist
doing the deed for me.

I have no excuse for what
I needed: to be
guilty.

After visiting a former lover in Manhattan,
I visited Liberty Clinic, swallowed the first pill,
its origins French as the famous green statue.

I used Mountain Dew to swallow the final pill
on the train for Coney Island. I say *Coney* when I mean
destination, the termination of pregnancy, the train ending
in a carnival, apart.

The gulls witnessed everything.
I stood on the boardwalk, marveling,
dumbstruck by dizziness as something left
this body, its warmth flooding my jeans.

My hands shook like toy airplanes.

No doula or doctor or nurse or friend intervened. No expert stood between
my breath and the sky,
my breath and the clouds, clotting,
my breath and the unwanted baby,
my life
      and the blood
on my hands, the certain solace,

    a choice
I made with myself.
I did it all.   I did everything.

I wore the silver mermaid necklace for years,
a souvenir

KERYGMA

The gun was his
idea.

Stretched over the front seat of his Chevy,
you found one lonely drum-stick

laid there amid rural lilies in stereo
surround, an arabesque

of loosestrife lines the ditch
of red dirt childhood

and you could be *anyone*
bending

to lift the apocalypse from
round your ankles.

But the gun must be his
idea, with you

going along for the ride.

For the kerygma of verge and virgin
sharing vowels, for the consonants

closing ranks
when his lips fall open;

you doubt his rebel yell,
the gun, his idea, nothing

special. Stretched over the front seat
of his South, past tense is

unspent casing. When the gun goes off,
you come in the name of

their fathers,
remember the blur of goldenrod.

CINE-POEM WRITTEN ON THE INNER ARM

after Benjamin Fondane

1. longing hides in a foreign body
2. taste of metal on the tongue
3. hint of blood, a panic bud, metallurgies of terror
4. form of love which doesn't seek to be possessed but to *belong*
5. cardboard box reaches towards a dresser drawer
6. safe text of citizened papers
7. child leans against mother-legs as bulwarks against erosion
8. longing survives her failure to keep soil in place
9. tree vanishes from the surface
10. roots reclaim their names by kneeling, digging
11. heart shaped like a shovel
12. child traces her silhouette with bare toes in the mud near a landfill
13. to make moms more than a rumor
14. men erased
15. rain came like mice to a cat's tongue
16. *listen: there is so much to taste*
17. an airplane shaped like Maria Tanasse
18. a home built of hunger named hope
19. the land we keep moving when cut by limits
20. night falls, blessed
21. night is the love we haven't met
22. night is all these borders, uncrossed yet

THE SKY LEANS OVER THE EARTH ON FOUR STILTS SPUN FROM STARS

begin in a public restroom
forehead flush against concrete,

the melody of beige
in the hands of a stranger
using the sink.

add the soap of no *doll-op*,
the sparkle of *nope* sounds.
a good-girl-poem waits

for the bass. the poem is
the fact's pain-ball, the burden
of verbing: you must write

a self out of waiting
to speak. the sky is your by-
line, a blue smudge

the god leaves on walls
when he's empty.
not even his Bigness

is free from wanting
skin in the son you made
for american cars.

i lie with your bullets
to comfort your guns,
confess to the wall,

the stall, these stars
tilt in relation to truth.

Sul Ponticello

The verb for longing in Romanian is a mouth-
ful of moist mountain soil.

      Our betrothal
      averted
            like eyes across a wooden pew
we divide
        what we must equal
     from the troth
            where swine sink their snouts.

Has it been years or
yards, fond ache-rage?

A fathom measures the distance between a pair of outstretched arms.
Still you hold me like jello
sul ponticello. On the porch,
in the kitchen, near a sink

sunset cannot overcome its habitual marvel:
gilded tongue, scalded marrow
I cannot linger
          far
behind your palm's urge

knowing
any body is a bow
tuned to tremble

tangled limbs, mottled
fruits, minor ninth.

MINOR NINTH

If I am here to sailboat, couscous, leather sandal, statue, raspberry gelato
then this museum is a mausoleum
in which our eyes tend to others

a rich crypt of unspoken poems

tick of tooth against tooth
the visible hunger a bridge
into books we read
coagulating in our blood

golden chasms
loblolly pines

don't say there is no forest
to a girl who never forgot

      the owl's call
      frayed noose
      being lost

remember amassing
darkness alone
between limbs

and the melodies you stitched
through insoles
leading me back

PROPER FUGUE

I feed the wrens, consider weather
and when to read your email.

Already, I am opened
                    up,

already I am struck by the shameless
hawk who dive-bombs between power
lines. Then rises to repeat his figure.

All movement is episodic, the gesture
subjects permutation. It is the absence
of wings that teaches us to walk.

And these words are not Bach, I know,
even birds develop hooves to move
through my head.

Once you knew,
                    too.

Once the flute turned to felt
in that piece by Sondheim.

I have learned so little
is a distance; the eye squints alone
over pages stacked with dim bars.

Each measure demands something new
from a sound; each stave expects his own
creme brûlée in Paris, his windowsill nude,
his film noir long-take, her exposure.

But the world did not end
when I studied your thighs
like scripture.

The sun failed to fall as we slept
on a broken sailboat in Cap D'Antibes,
when we made pillows from dirty shirts,
made love from couscous and pigeons.

The ground stayed firm
when I shaved my legs in the public fountain,
and this flesh,
                    this flesh
                so easy then, to rinse.

All music we found turned moat,
packing space inside a circling, the soak
of sudden threshold where

melody, like memory, crumbs
the trail of its undoing.

No singled subject resists
how struggle changes a theme.

The gentlest fugue begins in fear
of loss, and develops its argument.

No feast back to that first darkness:
your hands steadying my hips.

May this poem feed the forest
to fuel the fire I swore from rum
amid monuments, stone, explosives
one must ruin us.

The fugue of me cannot stop.

I have packed too much in
movement to measure the distance
between running and flying.

I fold this fire
into countless paper cranes,
and press send.

       Imagine your face, a wing,
       leave the rest to the winds.

IMPROPER FUGUE

allegro con fuoco

Does it irk you that the pool wears a silkier blue
at night? Lit from inside, like intimacy:

an incandescence edging nearer to
the underwater kingdom you imagined

before cartoons stamped castles on the vision.
Is the problem with light

       or what we call it

when a house intrudes, a barrier
holding the moon back from washing the lawn.

The city swallows whole stars, and exhales
them from smokestacks.

There was something I wanted from water
before you arrived, the wanting was

       mine. I love the blue

the way I loved the lit pool,
its lack full of promise, the impersonal

allegiance of longing, nameless-ed,
with no name to face or erase.

My Heart Like That Dress I Lost

Grey silk gown
entering an evening.

Once I wore you
to dinner with myself.

The pious silk of
your skin folded

between fingers, the
stranger pouring

any wine you wanted,
the fan blessing air

through a room after
copulation. We felt

everything choired,
partnered, twined.

That night we slept
on a beach. That dawn

we woke up alone
and in love with

the sun's scalded lips
opening then closing,

opening then closing
like blunt aubades

over us. I said one
was enough.

CHRIST INTERCEDES BY SHOWING GOD HIS WOUNDS

Iubitul-meu* approaches homework
with the brimstone of a lit fundamentalist:
each comma splices fresh

heresy. I caress him
with peach muffins
and bacon and beans.

I could not tender
the betrayed world
a rose from a poem
about punishment.

All executioners go home for supper
and no flowers stand in lieu
of what happened.

Now is infinite.
What's done is omnipotent.

I can't write to ransom
the crime from inside
the word criminal.

* *Iubitul-meu means "my lover;" the love & the beloved, inseparable, chained by a dash.*

LANDMARK STUDY

It was chaos or cherry tree season
when my aunt hung cherries
over my ears and said *earrings*

near the statue of Romulus & Remus.
It was Bucharest's compass, a sun-
central landmark for two-legged orbit.

It was the silk nightshirt I left
to embroider myself into his dreams
leaving no thread loose, as if

to provide the ideal is generic,
asking nothing absurd of the eye
apart from the absence.

It was noting an eye closes like tulips
without regard to the sun's position.

A tulip looks terrible dying.
This is the problem with writing:
everything hurts. I mean someone

is leaving, and the word for this
goes limp; the word plays dead
like an unstruck matchstick.

The plaza replaces the forest.
An airport arrives. It is too close

to comfort those who stay
marked inside others.

Only Mirrors

*The reason I speak time and again of poetry is that my whole life in prison
was infused with it. I had nothing. No paper or ink. The books lasted only
a short while. But in this vacuum I had struck a rich vein. Words. The force
of words. I had the words and I had the time. A huge amount of time.
Enough time not to know what to do with it. Time lost. But lost or not, this
time was mine. To allow it to become lost in vain was to lose a part of my life
and I wanted to live my life. With this joining of words and time I lived.
Survived. I even managed to be happy. Sometimes. I owe Mayakovsky a
great debt of gratitude.*

Lena Constante, a dissident who spent 8 years in solitary
confinement under the Romanian dictatorship for advocating
socialism with free speech and reproductive freedom

There are no curses: only mirrors
held up to the souls of gods and mortals.

Rita Dove, "Demeter's Prayer to Hades"

POEM FOR LENA CONSTANTE, ITSELF

Your prison diary hums through me
like acorns, a pinecone, fragments settled in audacity,
the possible is the quietest form of labor, industrious as the hermit
thrush who looms her nest through moments alone.

My world no longer reads itself without forcing
a fulcrum of fury into the line break, though good/bad guards
exist in most hallways, and the dungeon is there—below.
I keep the hope of you alive on its walls.

I copy your words along the wooden ledges of the kids'
bookshelf in black Sharpie. I believe the muscles of letters leave
irresistible witness to the world. The girl who loves words
must marry the books in her blood. The heart leverages

silence against the needs of the stadium, the shadows of forgotten
pietas, the iced light on the tree's holy vestments, a dog's bark
or pine trunk laid on my tongue in communion. Am I looking
down on the prisoner when taking her wound to my lips?

The torture, itself, what you called *the least* of it. Maybe
most is a route that knows ravage. It was your diary who taught me
to converse with my scars, those gaping seams on my knees, back,
forehead, scalp, the beautiful skull marked *safe*.

The body changes to reflect its relationship to the cell;
the barred light adds dimensions without erasing the object:
Itself. Meet me there, on the edge of what I've done.
I wait to dirge what cannot die, what waits for words in us.

My Polish Child

I lost a child on the streets of Krakow.

Somewhere near the center of the square,
women queued with pigeons.

The ending I wanted
was illegal.

My cousin came on a train
from Romania.

Like an accordion winding down a carnival,
we tried

hard to find the absent word. *Loss*
layered like velvet curtains
round our lips.

The cathedral held a rat
in reserve, its eyes approaching vermillion.

I felt a color. Not an expression
of life.

Stones steamed with the imprint of ancient chariots.

I crossed my heart, told my cousin: *we have always
been running, letting the next breath escape.*

A couple ended an argument under neon. I held tight
the ticket. What happened is unlikely

to explain. I must have carried it
wrong.

POEM FOR THE BEAUTIFUL SKULL

"Even blamed, your memory will live on in the legend of our country."
        [a note left on Ceausescu's grave by a visitor in 1994]

My mother's wild ghost still tingles my veins, her blood
laced with clotting factors.

I am with Eugen Jebeleanu in this beautiful skull,
the killer snuggles close as *nest* to *nestle.*

Near the ditch, I watch a hawk hitch a ride on a thermal,
suspended like the sudden vagueness among Romanians
when conversations inch back to the regime

        and verbs leave the mouth
wordless as hummed lullabies, melodies with lyrics
no one remembers.

There are terrors no American can tourist
in that Bucharest studio, the artist's fingers blurred yellow
by cigarettes, and dusk gilded the room in vintage-porn hues,
lighting a portrait of the artist's sister, a pianist & mother of five
        who died from an illegal abortion.

The artist cried, smoked, and survived
her own illegal events, seven total. She spat when she
spoke: *I don't believe in any man's protection.*
Women who trust male deities die of unrequited love.

I took the artist's tattered words into a small yellow chapel
and wrote them on the inside of my arm in black ink.
The text washed off in the shower
        but the dictator doesn't.

The dictator never dies
        in the throats of those who served him,
a god's name becomes a prayer.

Few resist.

In Alabama and Romania, the fear I found was a form
of service, a patriot's formal constraint.

Did I believe in benedictions when George
Herbert Walker Bush anointed Ceausescu
the good communist shortly after all abortions
became crimes against the Romanian state?

Did I believe in women helping women
when the Queen of England knighted the maniac,
and gifted her treasured hunting rifle to the dictator?

The man did not need a gun
to decimate an entire generation.

The beautiful skull waits for its ghost.

Men Say the Strangest Things to Me

Now I know the tardigrade lays eggs into a husk of dead skin.
I mean I gave him a soul that tasted like cinnamon cookies, but he wanted pound cake.
My face clear as a zombie's with no surface intent.
He says lambswool slippers and the house to hold them.
I said Trump is a racist.
I did not say his uncle was a racist who voted for Trump.
Kids in the ball pit are not blind to color.
The white girl hit her.
Colorblindness is adulting's professional erasure.
I still go for green Lifesavers and I did not lie when I said this nation is racist to the root-ball.
We shawl racism like winter in a French movie.
I am the problem on the family vacation where people vote Trump.
The gas tank ogles its empty.
An eye for an eye we have stolen from others.
Friends in big boots, what lie would you kill for?
The clumsy gait of the trombone aligns itself with elephants.
One dark night near the bridge where he leaves you.
I watch six braids bounce as the rondeau begins like elderfolk trampolining.
To be lost in the recital is to become the final note we expect.
Like "nothing" ever happens, we rue the invitation.
We can't budge without disordering the cosmos.
The clarinetist's long hair reaches down her shoulder and hardens into fuchsia.
To the man who inhabits each woman because he can't bear to live with himself, I say stop.
I drag this tongue down forbidden streets and call it a day.
Call it a blister, a mister, a frog who kissed her.
I wed the bed, reed the benchmark.

THINGS THEY CARRIED

Dear immigration officer, you were once a young fellow
that backpacked through Poland. Why the ICE now?

Dear spider, that's not your shoe. Dear foreign g-d, I don't
want to be any speakable color, to faux speak through skin

I didn't choose. If a voice implies a choice, I'm coddled
in silence. Dear palm tree, you look better on postcard.

You look best when we're not forcing yourself to shade us from
something. Dear Virgin Mary, you could be lying about

that hymen and still baking a Jesus in your belly. I know
the fun heft of raising an unplanned pregnancy, so heavenly

only a damned deity can do it. Dear mockingbird, you should
learn to ask for help. Dear sun, please stop burning my

children. The things we carried grow heavy enough to
hurt when they leave. To kill when given a backpack,

a mission, a gun. Dear womb, dear stupid little venerated
vessel: grow lips for the interrogation. What have we done?

QUAINT CONCEIT

I wake to cheap ontology,
the mouth's open wound,
recursive theme.

Rising action is a man's
room, a gunmetal voice
loading directions.

Once I took off my dress
for his shadow. It was
an apostrophe

before the rich bisque
of climax. A cauldron
of yearn I kept stirred.

I believe in fire as premise
of pyre to come. I believe
nothing lasts forever

but the ditch of amnesia,
the hollow a woman keeps
warm. Whatever a woman

keeps stewing for a hero
needs a home to leave,
a prize to win, a vaunted

arc of return. Is a rock
more than a surface
aching for lichen.

STRANGE ROOTS FOR LANDSCAPE

i.

The root of violence is *violation*, the fruit
of *viole* is the rape in Romanian. They say
victim but we force survivor in the States.
We levitate. We self-improve. We uplift
through talk shows & new kitchens.
We prefer no specific verb between
the self and its entertainment.

ii.

Violation, the last part pronounced *shun*,
the first of which is *viola*, floral umbrage
for a word that carries too much meaning
to manage *meaningfulness*. The blaring lack of it.
Like Alma Mahler carrying her ex-husband's
music scores across the Pyrenees when
fleeing the Nazis on foot. And how she lived
long enough to be blamed, to be shamed, to unknow every smile's assurance.

SINS OF THE FATHERS

The saints' tears are stored in a vessel,
a hollow vase resembling her body.

That prayer I want to believe
appears in a baba's nearing mutterances.

The problem is inflected, its knees
not wounded enough.

I have forsaken the sacrament of confession
for the pew of the poem, where
an inconstant angel of tinnitus
rules my right ear, demanding an ocean.

The babas are haloed by loneliness
as their men wait outside the church,
voices winding together like cigarette
smoke, the laughter of outdoor incense.

A baba tells a child this is why
her father's prayers go unanswered:
he never weeps for what he wants.
The sin is not in the desiring but
in refusal to beg for it.

What has no statue and yet
rules the world?

The poem is my penance.
The toddler is the daughter whose eyes
reproach my failure to preserve her tears.

But I kept your tiniest teeth in a silver box,
I tell the furious god in her,
I kept the hardness.

Time: When

And there will come an evening when I leave this place

And there will come a leaving when we survive the day

And a time will come when we die of hunger

And a hunger will come when we die of time

*

Italicized text is from Benjamin Fondane's *Simple Melodies*.

Plaintext is from Paul Celan's *Little Evening Book* where
Celan recorded wordplays & reversals in tandem with
Fondane's writing. These particular wordplays were dated
May 1, 1947, when Celan was preparing to leave Bucharest
for Vienna.

THE SONG IN MY EYE

after Ilya Kaminsky

A girl cannot live without her shadow.

I learn this in Romania from a peasant
who refused to walk past a new house
being constructed, or declined to stand
close enough to the house for the sun
to throw his silhouette upon it.

This is how shadows get stolen.
They are built into something else

I am so afraid of losing,
being lost.

There is a vampire in my left eye,
the one that is lighter,
hazel with yellow crumbs.

The sun conspires against me.
I tell my mom one eye is ruined,
one eye is not real, one part is mutt
or half-mutant, one view is a liar.

She bends, puts her knees on the
carpet to check, says it looks fine.

Says the eye is entire and
everything is fine and
the word for this is *lonely*.

My mom sings a song that uses her
hands to show me:

this is the church

and this is the steeple

now open the *dôr*

you'll find ourpeople

Against the Permanence of Portraits, We Posed Snapshots

for P.

I am holding a pinecone
inches away from your smile,
which is rising,
which is dropping the word *poise*
like a petal behind a bride,
leaving the parking lot altered
by vows and white flowers.
    Now I am thinking *our wedding*
with its November rain and live pig roast,
the mist made legit by silk & long trains
of lit in books feeling likewise.
    The noun possesses
what was felt without owning
anything, leaving the quick jazz
of suited hugs, the bluegrass of fist bumps,
the pop of giggles, the punk of eye rolls,
forsaking the field we promised,
wilderness, I can't
    remember.
A baked apple in the pig's mouth
rotating over fire for 24 hours prior
leaving our families, folded
into thank-you cards, leaving
the story to hatch again
    on a floored mattress
where dusk gathers round ankles
    like the fogged dress
I lifted like that bridge on the channel
that splits to make room for a mast,
for a sailboat, for metal's slow creak
    in the center, opening
the delicate spot we fear most
    may break
on an unremarkable morning
when called to bear weight.

Akhmatova's Gun

In the woods behind our first house, that picketless patch
of silence where we buried a precious yipper named Pinka,
seven years of christmas trees laid to RIP in the grip of kudzu,

I was thinking of the soul, that bow-legged buttercup, that big
Nothing which rose or resurrected, unless you count my wedding ring,
the whole fifty dollars of sterling swear-words I launched

into the woods' open mouth: the symbol you fished
out with rental metal detector. I was gathering my thoughts on marriage
being heavy as heartwood, a solid core buried deep in tree marrow,

thinking time is money we lack, as the climate of unscience
opinion keeps warming, permission to speak bites back like a mousetrap.
I was racking all this, and remembering why I love you

most honestly at night, after day has lost its voice, and everything
softens, how tenderness steeps like tea we must cool before tasting,
the steam of waiting you taught me. Keep teaching.

In the front yard, near the blight-hobbled dogwoods, the pennied
taste of panic thickening my tongue, I was thinking of the distance
between freedom and papers, how one thing in words

means running if you write it. I was remembering the soft
nose of our goat, how close it felt to the soul, that busted tulip,
the ground growing those incredulous ornaments without explanation.

PORTRAIT WITH PONY IN TRANSYLVANIA

The pony bit her close to the pelvis,
pale flesh of upper thigh going blue.

She kept the closed wound through
those two weeks they wandered,
the month of June's thickening bruise.

The love bite lingered like the scent of
old apples, your favorite perfume, the one
she wore when sealing gray ash inside
the middle blue matryoshka.

She carried the nibbling absence
over steep mountain hips, through streams
that dribbled like sweat between a landscape's
breasts. To find everything she adores
becomes a woman's body in her mind.

A man sold her beer named after
a bear and she drank it on the curb
where a road quilled into serpentine
as a story began to tell me.

An unplanned poppy queried
from the ditch—and what is memory
if not fondled ache, pony teeth,
cherished blister, budless thing,
unbound muscle sprain?

This wound with a hand
in its mouth keeps talking.

I carry your ashes in the blue
doll's womb. It is a tomb.
It is an ache. It is a train.

MEDITATIONS NEAR A TRANSYLVANIAN COOP

The kids chase chickens
then grieve for the hens
whose feathers are falling
from stress-induced events
including the rooster's
mating rituals.

The rooster looks hammered.
The hens watch the space
between the cock below
and the hawk above.

We watch the crower
strut the pen; wonder
when he'll give chase or
how long till he gets juiced
and pretends not to know
what he's doing & done
did etc. Two clouds
flex their alpine muscles
as my son finds a cat
on his tongue. My daughter
finds a puddle growing
its own rainbow. My hands
find the hen's eyes
blazed by hope's
avoidant pitchfork.

THREE WAYS OF WAKING

I wake up on the Liar's Bridge in Sibiu.

My skirt's on fire but my legs are freezing.

I wake to find my husband having a tryst in a labyrinth
that becomes a restaurant. The first clue is his decision

to sit at a separate table. Per the host's tip,
I have no choice but to seek him in the absence of maze.

In a labyrinth with only one pathway to the endpoint,
he screws a fake brunette on the formica counter.

I wake up in the Forest Without Fossils,
a land without memory of life erased.

There is a snake who knows the way, carving a soft
slither mark in wet soil, using his body as a blade.

There is a path that is neither bitch nor cherub.

I press my heart to the earth and crawl forward.

"Furesare:" A Conversation

In Moldovenești, it is customary to threaten some people like this: "Leave it to me to bring about your doom". One speaks these words to villains. If one wishes to cause someone else's death, one can take the following course of action. Fast for nine Tuesdays, not eat and not drink anything, during which one pays for a church service every week, where the priest reads Psalms 19 and 90, which list the curses of David. This custom is called furesare. The man targeted for that particular ill wish grows sick and dies soon after. Only a sorcerer who can figure out that the disease comes from some enchantment can only cure this disease.

—József Kádár, *Folclor românesc din nordul Transilvaniei*

The festive sorcerer lays gum on my right knee often. The molehill we make of mountains is majestic. The laurels we win for bold acts of ignorance is sweet tea, the ICEness, that conquest of killing strangers in chambers of illegible texts. Is bombing a hut the same as bombing a house if the hut can't score insurance? Ask the wizard. Ask the wizlet. Medusa, I kiss the lips you bare in the tree bark. The *furesare* is knit into the landscape. There is gum on my knee and smoke in my heart and most meteors are smaller than raisins. I will never eat grapes again. I'll go forth and savior the world with adamant hashtags and dragon-shaped craisins.

I : SAY : THREAD

The only grandmother   I ever met   wore the same emerald

silk dress   to all holiday meals.   Over a wingspan of decades

I grew   familiar   with the green and black spirals   swirling

round   her eminently foreign   body.   I say *Romanian*

because that's what she admired   when happening upon herself

in the faux   wood mirror   of her Alabama   apartment.

I say *luxury condo*   because that's what she called it.   I say *family* when

I mean   mirroring.   I say *silk*   because her eyes   ran

over   these teenaging shoulders   their tension.   Later, she took

the dress   back to Romania.   I say *infinite*   because she never

returned.   The last time   I kissed her,   she wore that   dress

in a casket.   In a chapel   where all lids propped open,   I say *silence*

because her lips   were stitched shut.   I say *Bunica*   because

that   is the word   for a woman   sewn into a dress   that loved me.

I say *loving*   because it is what's left   and   *forever*: too much.

So You Must Find a Way To Believe Me

I keep waking up and not trusting the coffee
to be real, to touch me.

      See, the squirrel with her nuts
      doubts nothing.

Even as the womb between our lips
buries terror into landscapes we have
lost, I won't

      Stop. There is so much to keep,
      moving.

I climb the nightmares to spite the mountain,
the mole-hill, the shitty logistics of girls
you loved, boys I tasted in library stairwells—

      All is luminous omen
      then gone.

The distance which slopes between
two bodies will keep its steepness

      In the image
      of a steeple.

Our daughters braid the tattered fringes
of carpet, name themselves after castles they need

      In some land we once
      read them to sleep.

Singular Accusative Forms

In Romanian, there is no clear distinction between objects, animals, and people for the third person singular accusative form....

Reapt

Pewed again, I admire Thy people
wearing ketchup on white-alert
collars. A baby awakes in the back.

Behold Thine retired cowboys, killjoys,
flock of long-suffering squawks.

O Formidable King of the Fabulous,
Thine congregants *in flagrante* stiletto
stay blessed with rhinestone hearts and emerald clavicles.

Everything is exquisite
excess. Even the golden eagle is litanous
and bizarre.

Intangibles can't damn us with their tinny
voices for Yours is the Vigor of Vigorousness.

Thou art the Hearer of Closeted Harks
who led a mouse to the trap this morning,
its curious jaws open wide as the eyes
of infants. It is in this way that I forgive
the debtor his interest.

I forgive myself, the faithless.

For the Monster of All Majesties fills us
with bread without revealing
the inhuman hand.

Lust Is Grief

Lust is grief that has turned over in bed to look the other way.
        Donald Hall

I could kneel in the hymn
of his hands dicing onions for *ciorb*a,
his version of my mother's soup
        softer than her
full-bodied original

Like Romanian spoken in a tunnel,
its diacritics muffled, strained into
        diminutives—something
emerges, diminished

    the accent on the end
of a word like *da*, the rising
pressure of affirmation,
        the promise to be pleased
when I am starved for a feast

only the dead
        can make
           Only the absent
can feed me, and no desire will match
this new knowledge of danger,
the unsettled, raw awe of it

     Which is not
like a thimble set against
        pricking but closer to the taste
of a copper penny given to a beggar
  not in passing
          politeness
but in the urgence
of one tongue
       touching
the border of another
leaving only money
in his mouth

Intensely, at Something

American Jesus was not invited
into the country of us.

It was no accident
we found each other like butterflies
who learn to read patterns of ultraviolet light
reflected from petals
to find pollen.

To find pollen
on our lips and foreheads,
the mark of hunger, recent
rapture.

Have you ever tried
to get inside the person you love?

     Keep going.
Desire is distinct, a way
of knowing. I needed
to shelter in place and be
known by a god who couldn't

unmake or revoke me, an unamerican
Jesus fluent in doubt.

Marked by pollen
we needed a nationless mesocracy
to marry us. In the cold

soil of November, that hush
between falling and freezing.

We couldn't know what would grow
there. We knew only
to hunt a limitless stanza,
a god, a poem, a lantern,

the lacrime* of landfilled dolls.

* *Lacrime* means tears in Romanian.

To Manly Muffin From the Mountainous Molehill Per Kids Today, Etc.

They let the lizard

        go near a drainpipe; four small bodies
        crouched round the motion of freedom,
        or what it feels like to children. Blessed

be that. And blessed

        be she who comes in the name of the
        Birmingham zoo's saddest lion, paws raw
        from pacing the cage. For peanuts

be freedom from

        knowing *zoos are for children,* preservation
        of exotic lil' species. I think I said this on
        the peak of said mountainous molehill,

my imagination

        doesn't work for money. It works for nothing
        and calls it luck. Don't forget this is the age
        of outraging outrage. Heartless self-help

is angina everywhere

        now. *Stoop down and drink and live,* a screenless
        voice said, its inflections the soft green of catnip,
        the watch-me-whip of wild violets, the lark-

spurring rainbows

        or riddles on tongues. The lizard is loose,
        pumpkin. Blessed be the teensiest creatures
        escaping castles reliant on captives of love

for money.

Disquieted Aubade

The morning after: a lip is a razor, an edge
to brush across a cheek, a partner in softening

       but I want to be a rock
       in the roadway, an obstacle

to my own company, styled like the monk's avoidance,
raptured in reams of black wool, a refusenik of

all fuckable beauty, unremarkable and yet significant
as the daisy between a week's unbrushed teeth.

The road careens as kids pretend to be quiet
as mice in the backseat, they play a game to survive

the imagination's cats, and I wish I could
drive with closed eyes and still keep

       this show whole,
       unwrecked, entire.

Dear man, dear god, your taste stays *glued* to my body
I cannot help playing along, inventing my own game

from monks whose silence forestalls settling into one
self, that series of solid expectations, the known

quantity, the serious waste of being a personality
outside the meter of interior mystery.

We pull over to pee in a meadow of yarrow and fire-
weed, I lay these lips on our kids as if they are mountains,

points of orientation on a pilgrim's landscape
whose only secret is water,

whose source may be the barren
stone cell that enables a monk

to unimagine this world out of
inconsolable longing to hear it.

Turbo-Folk Incident

for Jon & surreal confessionalism

I came to the park for songbirds
who sing in unpredatored darkness.

I was chewing on a man's finger-
pick, thinking banjo is new grass'

blueness. It was noonish & nowhere
near darkening. Me probing the notes

between agitprop & modes of remembering.
Yo nostalgia! Thou art stalwart in loyal

flashbacks & ads for kindred Coke,
the red wave flagrance. This is

how *we belong to a community*
in the commercial. My eyes go dirtier

than birders seeking the winged elusive
thriving in thickets with scarlet

underpants. I was still nibbling
this, chewing the man's pick

when turbo-folking happened.
The picnic shelter souped-up like

a Cadillac womb, its Avon flags aloft,
denizens sub-woofing local tunes about goodness

in greatness. Dirt for lyric nationalism,
days of goldens accompanied by subreddited

croon; being something is being part of
a package. Turbo-folksters hitched their

horses to neo-traditional conditionals
including plastics, jingo. One man

prep-ered to lay down his electric
accordion for the People.

It was like wishing on
screened stars, I felt connected,

directed towards the possible
cardinal, no songbird overheard.

I May or May Not Be Appropriate/It

I began the day with a word in my mouth
that absorbed every other word around it.
      Renee Gladman

I want to argue that this word in my mouth belongs to me in a way that cannot belong to the americanest poet. I want to explain how *ah-ZAH-Lay-eh* is different from azaleas as longing is different from *dôr* as a lullaby is a ghost's lingerie in another language & a curse when borrowed as accessory for the costume party. *I want to keep myself curled in italics.* I'm intrigued by the animal I can be in a zoo. I'm intrigued by love as the presence of absence, a sense of some-ing that persists in loss. I believe the word *dôr* includes this. I believe this belief is unique to me & therefore erroneous. Therefore as private as the ghost of my mother arguing with ice cream vendors in arboretums. I believe what is trivial will save what is not-me from myself.

WOMEN AT FORTY, ETC.

At forty, one knows why loneliness
wears the most spectacular diamond rings,
why Stevie Nicks' voice rattles like a shitty transmission
but never breaks down. The best engines are the worst, the wrecks
who strand us in a fisticuffs with stars, since we don't get raptured
like that on purpose. Though we will try. Good intentions know
what to achieve but not how to inhabit the body's raucous hungers,
to stroll the fine edge of not saying *now* when we mean something longer
than the sentence meant to hold it. Or the lifespan
it holds without intent. The distance between an urge and its splurge
is a summer parking lot, the sun warming shoulders with his
speech. At forty, one knows the heat kindled
by memory, the honeysuckle's first inch is
the sweetness. One knows what boys need to love
life is a bottle you pretend towards, a lie. And your sons
break hearts like boys broke yours, half-soused by
accident, drunk on astonishment. So one knows
how to be gentle with words, how to tender the cash of caresses
gone soft as meadows after rain, when soil smells
like the wettest part of love, and the moon is a promise
of silver in his eyes, bright cymbals, opening thighs.

"LIBERTY LEADING THE PEOPLE"

after Eugene Delacroix

The bulb beneath the bridge is broken.
It hangs from a pole, unfixed, unresolved,
ribald as foreplay French.

When I say never mistake
a poem for an etude, I mean depravity
wears rain boots in April.

I mean I found a toy accordion
but prayers still can't shorten
the accident's life, or seam

the scars' rotten memory.
We remember for money the lips
of the fathers, the lies of the sons.

The cold leche of marble counters
under my palm, the knife opening
the eyes of leeks.

A man without a home or family
knows the rich lie of our liberalism.
I share this wine freely with friends

but the mouth wants chocolate,
the mouth wants bayonet and bonnet,
bodice fallen to the waist.

SABOTAGE (OR SO MUCH FOR THE REVOLUTION)

as in *wreck* with slow hands, trawling the shores of my flesh,
marking the depth of each breath against buoyant prebuttal

as in *sinking* the writing I'd rather be doing than rising to meet
the loose tendon of words he tongues up my back, their soft demands

as in *deliberately damage* the muscles I tense against the gloss of girl mags
training me to please Him & blow Him's mind through the roof of parked cars

as in *cripple* with assumed consent until the ghost of my foreign mother
appears in her rosebud nightie, eyes narrowed like terrible hallways

as in *warning* me never to fake an orgasm, never cartoon the stars
or falsify groans, never xerox a moan onto your face

as in *destroying* your ability to feel is the curse of the fakers, the
women whose eyes get stuck in faux groans, artificial giggles

as in *vandalize* with teensy fib or false rib that teaches him to read
you wrong, an error he carries forward when he can't finish a book

as in *betray* with tiny scissors by lying to a man you want inside
you while staging the other lie to smoke him out

as in *ruin* the best question to pose before an aching body that
craves the shape his hands make of you, the lisp between quake and sky

as in *lie*: if I do, it is just to say I am still my mother's daughter,
to say dear america, I can't fake it to make it work.

Minor Major Seventh

A bench establishes distance from the piano,
makes solid the space for knees.

Among minor things I should have felt but failed
to flesh: the turbid half-light on the seam

of his lips, two lines on a road, never crossing.

It was the snail and shell of things, the hard
softening of broken staccato

as I veered between trope and tribute,
the verbs weakening into satin,

swearing *dawn, window, dolor*…. I should have told you
all flowers die young, and nothing gets older

than the song one wants to resist. The dinner
expects something from the ghost.

The bench stays pulled back, avoiding the nocturne.
The majority of daylight fades into shades

of fakeness. A neighbor swears love is permanent
while packing her van for Disneyland.

Apologetics in a Modern Key

Judas visits me in a daydream on the playground; my children arrange mud pies to bake in the sun. I don't know how he could avoid betraying Christ once Jesus predicted it, once a prediction becomes divine mandate issued by Eternal Daddy. *Put that stick down*, I warn my daughter, myself. Aren't we all the same question at some point? If there is a plan, it may end near the swingset. Reductionists clearcut the forest to make sense of the trees. The mud pies dry, the dirt crumbles until it enters the moisture of mammalian mouth. We remake mud by eating the food shaped from the ground. If Judas didn't betray Jesus, then God would be so dead wrong.

Deep Fake

*Be careful with plump, drinking Russian women...You just do not know
how far they might go out of that stupid Russian patriotism. But I know.*

> Svetlana Alliluyeva, Stalin's daughter speaking to a
> Western journalist who mentioned visiting Russia in
> the early 2000's just before she warned he might be
> kidnapped by Putin

My teen son thinks *hurt has gone deep-fake*: an image altered by trolls,
propagated by Russian bots. He says this because suffering feels privileged

on a planet where sadness is a crime against positivity, humankind stays
medicated and never sober. My son is somber when he picks his nose

because we won't stop fracking the earth and it's absurd to talk manners
mid-planetary-rape. Three years ago he forgot the final note of a sonata

and no one at the recital noticed. *They clapped even louder*, he says, this is
why he will never believe us: the audience dressed for adulting as the devil

bakes meth at the ballpark when a toddler shoots Mee-Maw in Wal-Mart
while a teacher sexts her anus to a teen quarterback whose brother is dying

of cancer. In places we can't discuss, my son believes we're lying through bones
that bleach teeth. I hustle hope into hugs, hold out for peak fake to come.

MONOCLAD

I think you know what glibness protects.

In all memories revised by your mother's failure
to be the thing you needed, there is the   thing
                            you will be.

There is the *thinging* of it.

When your daughter says you ruined her
life. You may wish it were so, wish any life

                was yours
                    to spoil rotten
                    and marinate in worry

         before releasing a girl into the world
                         with that greed.

For love. For need. There are two
sides of a room but one absence
makes them equal.

Intense light fools the eye
by resembling darkness.

What is bright deprives the vision of an image.

It is kin to pitchblack in this loss
of sight. Both remove the mind

from its bearings.
            I saw a bird before the truck
            hit me, or imagined
            what I must have seen
            after.

I think you know how waking
shapes both nihilist and ideologue.

SAY DUSK WAS OUR COUNTRY

for C.

Was it a garden or a landfill?

You read Parfit as I smoked clematis.
Dusk laid her demands on the brow of a hill.

Shadows love burdens, you said, brewing
coffee. Nightingales sing all night, spilling their songs
straight through sunrise, to stay alive

is to keep from sleeping.

Darkness asks a certain vigilance of its initiates
but the invisible never diminished us.

I am still famished, unfinished
by dimness. Each ache, the open arm of ellipses,
light withdrawing her gaze

from liminal spaces. And every moment
holds one bidden thing back.

I forgive life for ruining Wittgenstein, Foucault,
those safe suburbs of logic; remember carving mud with your Civic,
wheels spinning, our mouths howling Pixies lyrics,
our heads uncombed by failure or success.

How I craved what your mind did to mine, the minor
miracles we bore like tin soldiers, ontologies blazed on cereal boxes
like a trail of hearts on parole from holies.

And I am still restless, rambling, hunger-faced,
still ogling starbreaths for the right story.

I miss you & I, too, forget me.

Pitch a tent in the nearest meadow.

Lay your lips on any scarecrow who speaks.

Relapse

Every elegy always conceals the hope that the miracle it celebrates, the miracle of someone's life, of some event, will come into being once again...A poem's mystery is always ahead of us.
      Adam Zagajewski

In the car bleary-eyed. We down-shift
past a dying bird. The struggle to untangle
broken bones, steal a step forward.
What life believes death when it arrives?

A desert monk named Agathon
lived for three years with a stone in his mouth
so he might learn
to keep silent.

When we return to a space without words,
it is a relapse. Rise from bed with an image
of mom, remembering the image is all
she left. Bitter buzz of whiplash, a *was*

a was wuzzing. Stages of grief are closer to stadiums
where we sit and engage the world, schools where we learn
to spectate. Even if death is nothing which happens on stage

but a galaxy we can't see beyond.
Maybe these are different
doors and I am starved for
a label.

Suicide: a door that closes us.
Euthanasia: a door we ask others to shut, a story
about consent & how we honor other bodies.
And something else: a mother's death,

unspeakable as exquisite sex, *unfathomable* ravage.
The knot and ruin of a good life.
The bird's wing. The beak's crunch.
The innocent blizzard.

Setting My Bed on Fire

We draw a wall. We glue
snakes to trees. I'm deaf.

In my youth I held incorrect
opinions. I'm dying and

setting my bed on fire. It's creamy.
I'm eternal, death says.

Tomaž Šalamun

LITTLE TIME

We must go for a walk
in the freshly-washed
world, he says.

We must venture into
the thicket with cacti
in our open corneas.

There is so much to see,
little time.

Little time, trickling from an eave.
Little time, dropping from leaves,
falling, collecting, becoming
serious puddles for
paper boats to cross.

We must build a paper-boat
in the freshly-puddled
world, he says.

We must write our secret
names on the hull.

Little boat, braving the wavescapes.
Little time, before water softens paper.

Was it earlier, a newsman reported
a young mother's body washed
to shore during the storms.

I imagined her shoes,
little boats.

The newsman spoke to us.
He said: *And now, way ahead
of time, she was gone.*

A LUSTRATION

Lustrate comes from the Latin verb meaning "purification by sacrifice;" the process of making something clear or pure by means of a propitiatory offering.

In politics or law, *lustration* refers to the restoration of a government's credibility by the purging of perpetrators who committed crimes under an earlier regime.

*

Inside every word hides an argument: a jury of dim alleys.

The wind it was. The tin trash lids percussed. A choir of oak limbs bore witness to the lustration of dor's first body.

One one trembling matchstick; my hand
in the night of it, knowing longing grows stronger in withholding
its initial draft.

The cloud mass that wanted to rain met its match
in the lack.

The manuscript's cremains, softer than lover's skin
after sex; I tucked them in

to her wooden box.

A mountain carved over
the top. See, we could not arrive without a fire,   You & I,
without burning a book to bring

this one to life. The lustre-monster of ash
shelved, the book stacked
near an urn with
mom in it.

OVID AS A BRUISE

You will be separated from yourself and yet be alive.
Ovid, *Metamorphoses*

To lose a country is to let go of the known
for the dread zone on a map.

The alien sculpts new verbs in navigation,
she coins nouns to accommodate

dislocation. In the AP history classroom,
you may caption the fable she owes

this country, the belt shaped like a smile
cannot move. A statue collaborates

in her silence. A rock can't risk roots
in longing for a place of origin.

The word for *missing* becomes a bruise,
the hidden bloom in a stone's mouth.

Ancient Greeks believed exiles were liars,
lacking loyalty, traitors to the language

that made them. Ovid's statue gazes away
from Constanta, the Romanian port of his

banishment. I see him staring over the ocean,
seeking legibility: a salve for his divided

body, words bouldering like a bridge
between the eyes of two harrowed lovers

holding intimate the abortion between them:
a dream so treacherous they chose

to kill what they'd imagined
                              to survive.

Red Chair with Potential

I stared at the red chair until
it turned into a boulder in a chestnut
grove where dolls remove their
clothes and cry. But first, it was

a podium where the blond Barbie
pastor officiated a marriage of
two moms. Then it was a hide-out
for horrible toothaches. Look,

I don't believe my mom knew
she was dying, or I need to prove
none know the difference between
dreaming & disappearing, its edges
sunk like the angles of shipwrecks.

The bottle near the boulder
has no message. The chair is
never a constellation. I give up
on the moon, its bold statements,
all boneless promises, meat.

There is a mask inside
a man on the bridge before
dying. There is the water.
There is a way falling goes
on without us. Pretend
it's the boulder.

WITH MY HEAD LEANING OVER THE SIDE OF THIS

I laid in my childhood
room
          where boys & stars felt the same

distance apart
                    from a head or the hole in my bed.

In my bed, it is better to be used
than indicted
                by the uses
                 knotted into   one's body.

It is best to be a folded
pajama that emerges for the
lullaby's snake-song.

I need something elusive
as a lyre about moonbeams,

an imaginary muscle that leaps
the creek
          into a language
                          that leaves you behind.

In my head life begins
with a tadpole, a sapling, a monk's magic beard,
your eyes, the coin bartered with water
for wish, a homeland
                        of oak roots
                        who ravage the lip of a sidewalk,

destroying all property values.

Maybe justice will damn us.

Please god
erase every   thing
I want   these trees to win.

NOCTURNE WITH A BOTTLE OF HOME-BREWED TUICA

We won't argue geopolitics, or up antes for whose fetus felt
        saddest first. Since the vast majority of thighs

devise lyric from ruins, we won't force remorse. On the porch,
        one lonely rocker flirting with wind

as streetlights bow out, the sky insists on opaqueness.
        The sunflower's head hangs from a stem.

Art can be mixed up in anything, given light. We mint love
        from verbs that won't budge when what we see

is not *felt*, not the onset of velvet's elaboration. The babies
        sprout teeth and start strolling but the brick

at the building's base remains the hardest to paint.
        In the land of unknowing, you hold my name

in Romanian, making a home. So that is our house, and
        you are my spouse, my hubcap, my favorite guise.

Night serifs our faces in owl thoughts but darkness contrives
        no distance. You know my shadows and desolate habitudes,

the slant of my throat, the mouth that opens, the jugular note
        of the nocturne that develops from dropped kudzu vines.

DISCARD

Autumn alters the hue of matins;
dying tastes akin to the timbre of
rotting leaves. The pitch of bleak
tar painted on fence posts, a device
to administer the intimate. Each dawn,
the hummingbird kick-starts her heart
at 500 beats per minute, the slope
is the steepness, or why many die
in their sleep. A yard's fastest heart
is untenable as the poem reaching
toward a wound, all verbs, basteless.
Even this verse is a tunic someone
wears to watch birds. It is nothing.
They are children, the toy's soiled
detaching limbs. I hope anyone
accused of my life will be remorseless.
To grieve and yet believe this is how
the poem works, in shifts and brief
shakings, in fits and repeats.
It is the flip and the flop-
jaw, the bullet's open bleak,
the steepening commitment.

ON LOVE AS RELIGION WITH SPECIAL WAFERS

Plankton are small, feebly-swimming
creatures located inside an ocean.
You are the light of the world,
dear man, you are the wick in
me. This is a collect for purity
with diatoms for eyes.
Oil is lighter than water.
Toes are lighter than tummies.
The sun rises with hidden
ropes each morning. Marine life
is sorted by lifestyle, whether bottom-
dwelling, top-oriented, or dogging
the middles of all I can think
when you swear it
is easier to be from somewhere
else. You are the light of the
world and plankton is your bitch.
At the mercy of tides for transport,
plankton is wary. You are the light
who says holding my breath
makes it harder to control it.
I am *your welcome* when lit.
It is uneasy to be anywhere
that keeps moving.

REVISITING THE ROMANIAN REPUBLIC OF ALABAMA

I've returned for the letter you must have written
to absolve all serial-killer cabbages in my dream.

Living with your death is a nightmare I can't evidence
without you. Did you teach me to build a country

I've forgotten? My husband hates rolling *sarmale* alone.
This whole scene is raw kitsch and untenable:

take the broken bottle-blonde in the mirror,
a long trail of ashes climbing into her mouth.

Take the kids who call this doll *mommee*, ladle them
lentils. Things have changed since I stomped through

the unofficial republic of diacritic azaleas in combat boots
and all-black. I kept my face like a Modigliani until you fed me

cobbler, and said: *Nu-ți face griji, sweetie. Hating yourself is so lux
only americans find time to do it.* I'm wearing your too-small

sandals looking for bones you must have left. I'm talking to t
he ladder, the moon-vine, the statue of someone's nose, the echo

of your cackle in the study beside the gold crucifix
whose head toppled off, stayed lost, the gamut.

I am losing this wanton mind near the dogwood where
I lost my punk Barbie, just before the bed where I abandoned

a virgin tongue when she ran out of stories worth reading.
I'm still reading myself into things, including gunshots,

glaucoma—my family says I'm the frostbite no toes believe
in a desert. On a planet with no map to hold me, I'm still waxing

my legs with wine & laughing before crying wins out, like you
showed me. I'm still strolling the hairballed rugs of your hallway,

running recon with the armored commas of family portraits.
I pause to kiss the semi-colon aunts, to lick the babas, to icon

the drunkest uncles. I miss the land your arms made me.

I can't quit looking, flexing the myth's little muscles as if
to ask what follows from absence and how, mamica   *how*

Dorință

(noun) a desire or wish. A form of dor that includes all the others; an accumulative cento; a self-centograph; a poem sewn from lines in previous fondles; a summation that arrives at the word, dorinta,; the wish of a wish; an index of longing; the cenotaph-cradle of italics to carry ghost lines of poems removed from the manuscript: the traces of what almost happened; the repository of all dors priors; a homeland in my head.

I lay my head on the map that can't hold me. The sky is desert with a stone in his mouth. The light of the world is my heart in the word *revolution* lying sideways. My soul limns an un-american fluent in doubt. We come from the dreams of small children, feeling *scarecrow*, knowing *empty*, eating Legos to make a point about pointlessness. The bravest babies fight cocks & bold roaches for bread crumbs near the beak's crunch, past the mountainous molehill. *I have a poor spirit*, I told the beer named after a bear as *lindens staggered through crypts.* Dear Alabama, please stop burning my hope-work. Dear Sun, the babas are haloed by brambles: one version of *lonely* in the bluegrass of fist bumps, the hot punk of eye rolls, the innocent blizzard. The problem with writing is everything looks terrible dying, and the poem wants the bodice, the church, the steeple. The dictator lies on the lips of those who served him. Things we carried grow heavy enough to hurt when they leave. Losing is belief in its bewilderments. With diatoms for eyes, I keep myself curled in italics, nourish this lie on the lawn, the hush between falling and freezing. I was thinking of the ghost, that bowlegged buttercup, meter of interior mystery. The danger is not dying but *living in exile from longing,* from knowing the name of what is gone. Each frack or fuck on the planet seeks a mermaid; each love, a book or wren. *I took off my dress for his shadow in the origin of roses.* The poem is the fact's pain- ball, the sunflower's head hangs from a stem, the noun possesses what was felt without owning the chair. The sky blesses the boots I've worn to stomp out of the house I've become under neon. Lit from inside, I ladle ashes from the lustre-monster's mouth. *My hands are magnolias, sparrow vespers, oak limbs* the fugue of me cannot stop the fire. All hurt is *american carnage.* The skulls fake it to make it work.

Notes

+ The portions of text in italics are direct quotes from Emanuela Tegla's endnotes to Petre Solomon, *Paul Celan: The Romanian Dimension*, published by Syracuse University Press in 2019, for which Tegla served as translator. The non-italicized portions also borrow heavily from Note 14, found on page 193.

Early Doinas
Epigraph is from Varlam Shalamov's *The Kolyma Stories*. Shalamov was arrested in Stalin's great purge of 1937 for having declared Nobel laureate, Ivan Bunin, a classic of Russian literature. He spent nearly seventeen years in the Siberian prison camps. "Like A Fire of Suspicious Origin" is titled after a line in Nicole Sealey's poem, "A Violence." And "The Communist At Catholic School" is dedicated to Zach Doss, who believed in it, and whose light remains.

Dynamite
Epigraph is from Benjamin Fondane's *Existential Monday: Philosophical Essays* (New York York Review Classics, 2019), translated by Bruce Baugh. "Cine-Poem Written On the Inner Arm" follows Benjamin Fondane's unique cine-poems into a different tense, a loose future anterior. "Christ Intercedes By Showing God His Wounds" is written after and with Zbigniew Herbert

Only, Mirrors
Epigraph from Lena Constante's *The Silent Escape: Three Thousand Days in Romanian Prisons* (University of California Press, 1993), translated by Franklin Philip with an introduction by Gail Kligman. Communist regime carefully destroyed artists, writers, and intellectuals by prison and death camps and later by censorship, threat of death, and lure of reward. Rather than focus on legal guilt for particular crimes, the regime kept citizens afraid and ruled by terror—fear of saying the wrong thing and being overheard, since a casual joke was enough to result in a camp or prison sentence. Anyone could be a threat. Any day created a new list of possible traitors. Self-policing corroded popular trust in the relationship between word and deed. Romanians lived divided. At Pitesti, where Constante spent time, the prison was revealed as a means of re-educating political persons into compliance by breaking them down, forcing the tortured to become torturer, creating a web of complicity in which all hands were dirty, and all were damned. The line which designates

criminal from official is always slender, shifting shapes, and reflecting on the culture of carceral injustice.

Singular Accusative Forms
"Turbo-Folk Incident": Turbo-folk music emerged as a recruiting tool that engaged young persons to fight in the nationalist Balkan wars of the 1990's.

Time, When
Epigraph is excerpted from Petre Solomon's memoir, *Paul Celan: The Romanian Dimension*, published by Syracuse University Press in 2019, and translated by Emanuela Tegla.

Setting My Bed On Fire
The epigraph is from Tomaz Salamun's poem, "Who Doesn't Hide Behind the Altar."

"Men Say the Strangest Things to Me" is a monostich sequence inspired by francine j. harris' expansion of Robert Hass.

Acknowledgments

I don't have words for all the gratitude I want to lay over the editors, first readers, and mammals whose late nights include creating the following literary journals where some of these poems first appeared—and to those editors who nominated some of these poems for prizes, or who awarded these poems prizes, or who sent a smiley-face emoji in an email on a day when nothing was working—you are an astonishing light in my life. And I am so grateful.

Apofenie: "Poem for Lena Constante, Itself"
Barren Magazine: "My Mom & Her Monks"
Boston Accent Lit: "Relapse"
Crab Creek Review: "I : Say : Thread"
Cortland Review: "My Heart Like That Dress I Lost"
Dishsoap Quarterly: "Red Chair With Potential"
EcoTheo Review: "Reapt"
Exit 7: "Cosmology"
Free State Review: "Against the Permanence of Portraits, We Posed Snapshots"
Ink & Nebula: "Women At Forty, Etc."
Journal Nine: "On the Second Day in Transylvania"
Mantis: "Minor Ninth" & "Kerygma"
New World Writing: "With My Head Leaning Over the Side of This"
North American Review: "Unamerican Litany" (finalist for 2019 AWP Ron Brown Prize)
Pleiades: "The Song in My I" & "Little Time"
Pocket Samovar: "Pickled Plums" & "Doina For What They Did," originally "I Keep Flashing Back"
Poet Lore: "Failure to Conjugate"; "Men Say the Strangest Things To Me" (nominated 2019 Pushcart Prize)
Porterhouse Review: "Akhmatova's Gun" (finalist 2019 Porter House Review Poetry Prize)
Prairie Schooner: "Playing Possum"; "Me & the King"; "Sul Ponticello"
Qwerty: "Deep Fake"
Rise Up Review: "Liberty Leading the People"
River Heron Review: "Proper Fugue" (Winner of 2019 River Heron Review Poetry Prize)
Southern Humanities Review: "Things They Carried"
The Citron Review: "Sabotage (Or So Much For the Revolution)"

The Mississippi Review: "Intensely, At Something" (finalist 2020 Mississippi
      Review Poetry Prize)
Twyckenham Notes: "So You Must Find A Way To Believe Me" (Second Prize,
      Joe Bolton Poetry Award)
Up the Staircase Quarterly: "Three Ways of Waking"
Virga: "Lust Is Grief"
Whale Road Review: "My Polish Child"

Gratitude

Hot-mic hugs to the local poetry reading collective that welcomed me to Birmingham and in whose company some of these poems began, including Laura Secord, Ashley M. Jones, Joi Minor, Tina Mozelle Braziel, Lauren Slaughter, Octavia Kuransky, Sanovia Muhammad, Maria Vargas, Lori Lasseter Hamilton, Salaam Green, and others. Special thanks to Bread Loaf and all its wonders, including Jennifer Grotz, and to Matthew Olzmann and Vievee Francis, who inspired endlessly. Additional thanks to Kwoya Fagin Maples, Amelia Martens, Erin Coughlin Hollowell, Matthew Olzmann, Jihyun Yun, Emily Holland, Clara Burghelea, and Ioana Hobai. A whole entire heart to Heather Durr, who stitched a quilt with the words from these poems and mailed it to me, thus opening a gift of light in the pandemic week after I received scary radiology results and lived in the limbo between lab tests and surgeries, curling into this blanket (I believe) is the fabric-garlic that protected me. My forever love to Pamela, Doru, Carla, Jeremy, and big kisses to Isla and Lydia, whose laughter is a chime I hold close, and to Vicki, for the doors she taught me to keep open and the love tended behind them, and to Sanda, Filip, Remus, Alice, and Mop, for mititei, love, and laughter. One gargantuan heart for Patrick, for all the reasons he is and all the reasons he knows, and three diamond hearts for Micah, Milla, and Max, whose dances, invisible horses, and petit princes light my life (I am so grateful to be your mom-ster, always). And last heart for the love I keep for ghosts, Mom among them, dancing to Leonard Cohen for eternity.